Barbed Wire and Bailer Twine

The Complete Book

by

D. Manderston Mackrill

Sponsored by The Nestle Company Ltd.

First published in 1992
by
D. Manderston Mackrill

Springfield Farm,
Baldhu,
Kea,
TRURO.
CORNWALL. T.R.3. 6.E.D.

I.S.B.N. _______0.9517767.0.3.

FOREWORD

This is a book of great charm and originality. Humour is never far away. To use David's own term he "paints pictures in words". These "pictures" are tremendously evocative. They make you see things through his own "green" eyes. You rejoice at the peace of the old pony resting under the oak tree. You grieve as the old hedge is destroyed. You smile at the creaking of the Little Grey Friend. You get a sense of excitement as the twigs snap when the badger is rooting for food. You feel with the author when the words "disintergrate before his eyes".

His love of words has survived his schooling. Few people then could understand that someone whose spelling was not decipherable was in fact, intelligent and had a great feel for the language he could not express on paper. Some teachers covered his books in red ink and assumed he was "thick". A few looked beyond his spelling and argued his intelligence. The result was that, going to the opposite extreme and ignoring his problem, he was entered for eight 'O' levels. He failed them all because his written work did not reflect his knowledge.

It is a long way from eight exam failures to having a book published and only David will know just how much courage and will power it has taken to get there. He is an outstanding example of someone whose determination and persistance have enabled him to overcome the dyslexia which he had to a severe degree, and to manage any residual difficulty. This book must be a beacon of encouragement for those struggling with their dyslexia and for David, an Everest conquered, an ambition achieved. Those words in bold letters on the cover will not disintegrate -
D. MANDERSTON MACKRILL

HELEN ARKELL
PRESIDENT HELEN ARKELL DYSLEXIA CENTRE

David finds many ways to spell any word. His cows dont get concerned by this, but, for this book the spelling has been corrected, and rewritten, again and again.

David, being David, there are still some words spelt incorrectly.

This somehow seems to add to the magic of this book.

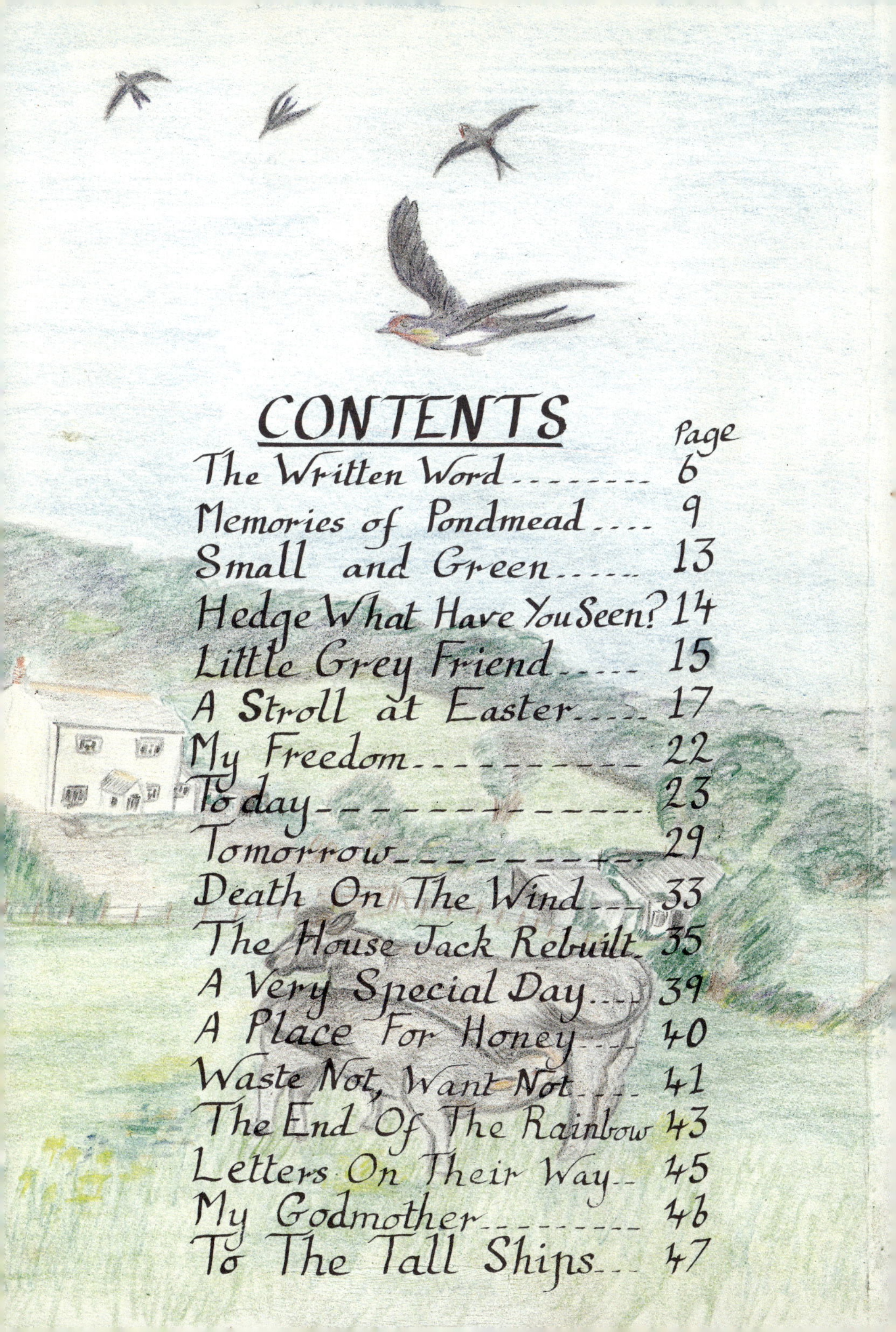

CONTENTS

The Written Word

I try to read and write,
Tell left from right,
Pass exams all right,
Use the pen to fight,
Out comes the word,
Then disintegrates before my eyes.

Books; little letters,
Metered across the page,
Like a jigsaw awaiting to be made,
A group here, a group there,
A pattern begins to form,
Then disintegratates before my eyes.

Learning goes in the ear,
Stays a while, may stay on,
Or, on its way may go,
I recall, and try to write,
Which word to use? I know,
Then disintegratates before my eyes.

Head empty of the written word,
Colour and sound become sharpenad,
To solve the problem, rethink again, again,
Unaware of the pregudice of the written word
Each thought, new and clear,
Then disintegrates before my eyes.

Grey newspapers lie open,
Magazines, bright and gay,
Their sheets eraticaly dotted,
With pictures of yesterday,
Groups of letters, making words,
Then disintegrate before my eyes.

I can hear the nightingale sing,
I can smell the fox,
I can touch the grass,
I can taste the food,
I can see the written word,
Then disintegrates before my eyes.

Memories of Pondmead

Bewitched by time, remembering when the air smelt of lavendar, as the sun forever shone.

An acre of heaven, apple blossom, newly mown grass, shaded by a giant walnut tree.

The small white cottage, snuggling, bulging with love, oak beams, trying to hold in the walls, as the smell of oatmeal biscuits drifted on the breeze.

Tucked in one far corner of the garden, the old pigsty, now housed a new occupant. Green and black, with shining brass; to perfect scale, many years work, reproduction in miniature, "The Little Bear" steam engine, built by William Watt Izzard, picture restorer, framemaker, inventor; achieved his dream. Puffing down to the tobacco plantation in the other far corner. The hands of my Grandfather had created the dream of any young boy.

Sheltering under apple, plum and pear, looking out over the lily pond, stood a fairy like summer house; inside a handmade oak chest, along side wicker chairs. Think of a game, dream, wish; open the chest and the wish, came true.

Overshadowing all but the walnut tree; the creosoted barn, used as a workshop, apple store honey in the pot; while hanging high in the roof lines of drying tobacco leaves, like kippers. Gold leaf, carefully placed on hand carved frames, as artists paint mixed its perfume with the rest, making an unforgettable cocktail.

'I was not yet ten'

My grandparents,
Mr. & Mrs. W.W. Izzard.
His "Little Bear"
Steam engine.

Early in the 1950's
at "Pondmead"
One of my early photo's.

The old shootingbreak patiently waited, just inside the large doors.

Looking to the Chiltens, on the way back to the cottage, high up in the clouds, to heaven, a gold ball, balanced on a granite monument, glinting. Telling the world of my humble grandfathers abilities, a craftsman among craftsmen.

Inside the cottage, neat and proper as if still running her school, my grandmother, firm but loving; brought mahogany, oak and gold, set in these white walls; to life. Whilst the scent of lavendar mixed with the sweet smell of apples and oatmeal; your eyes feasted on the work of craftsmen from Japan, Africa and Persia, as well as Europe, often restored by my grandmother's needlework and my grandfathers skills.

Stairs; dark, whitchelm, sculpted by hand, fanning their way up to beds, soft enough for a Princess.

Looking out at night across the meadow, dark shape of the hills light up with a glow; the "Flying Scotsman" was climbing the Chilterns. Bewitching me, as I slipped into the world of dream.

Small and Green

On my little farm; away from subsidy and profit margins. Enjoying the badger and the fox; foxgloves and buttercups colour the hedgrows in the fields. The old pony sees out his days under the spreading oak; the cattle still tell me of the oncoming rain. Trees lean out of the wind, and the grass grows taller in the lea of the hedge.

Cows graze, calf at heel; as the sun sets fire in the West. Hedges of holly and hawthorn, caught by the rays, show off their crops in glory, to tempt the birds to feast.

Before the coming of the night, the badger and the fox; mice scurry under twigs on the hedgerow. Rabbits graze amoung the cows. The bracken is dry, crisp, cracking as a badger roots for food.

But; to the East; the fields are green with nitrogen; hedgerows neat and trim. Standing like scarecrows at regular intervals, lone wind-swept trees. The tall green field, uniform in colour, blown by the wind, makes waves as if at Sea.

Oxen graze up to a line; pulled tight, straight across the field. Brown earth and mud, around their water trough; where they push their huge wallowing bodys forward; like elephants at a water hole.

Only grass to eat, for months on end; then corn, like chocolate every day. No room for buttercup, thistle or worm. No seeds for the bullfinch; no place for the mouse, only pigeons for the greens.

Hedge, what have you seen?

What man has passed this way since, branches layed where covered in earth to make a wall, leaving a ditch to drain, each year a little deeper, each year a little higher.
For so many years, you have stopped the gale.

Did you see the tanks go to war?
Miners pass this way, or Kings hold court, in autumn chill?
When did the holly, oak and hawthorn grow, did the badger cross this way before the cavalier, how many times did you shade the smuggler on his way?
Animals graze your banks, birds eat your fruits. Did you see the Romans march this way? I heard King Arthur my have gone that way.

Gone is the hedge, to stop the wind.
Gone are the banks so green,
Gone is the holly, the oak and the howthorn.

The mechanical digger; so strong, to push the past; right away.

Hedge, whot have you to say?

Small, one acre fields, date back to 2,000 B.C. the end of the "Stonage".

Little Grey Friend

I have a little grey friend, stands about fourteen hands; sits for weeks on end, through rain or shine, works all day without a neigh.

Pulls plough or cart, the same. When cold, will puff with joy, to come to life.

Tread now a little worn, the grey a little frayed. Saddle worn, and joints a little slack. My little grey friend, will purr along road, across field, through wood, or by the sea.

He does not hesitate to lift, half a ton for me, or pull three times this up a hill.

Through Fifties, Sixties, Seventies, on he goes, Eighties nearly gone. Summer heat and winter cold, purring through the seasons.

From the stable of Standard, his pedigree, without doubt pure Ferguson, My little grey friend, so dear to me.

A Stroll at Easter

That small village, not far from Matlock; as the night drew in early, it being the eastern side of the Pennines.

Like a lone centurian, the village policeman peddled along his beat.

Bleak, grey and snow covered, where centuries before, the Romans marched. Grey, small, houses, sheltered between dry stone walls.

Some hours before, we had been in the centre of England, beside nineteenth century roads of water, where the twentieth century built towers into the sky...... A chariot had left Bob and I in the outback of the Roman Empire, to be questioned, by the centurian..... We were now trying to convince an unbeleiving officer, that we were students from an agricultural college in Surrey, over one hundred and fifty miles south. Straight, cutting, each question, like a sword searching its mark. Answers, reflecting the blows, telling how, with five shillings (25p), that Easter weekend, in the early sixties; we were racing to the bright lights of Blackpool, and back to college. On request, we lifted our feet from the frozen ground, to bare our souls, to this unbelieving guard of society....satisfied; he was unable to stick us with any crime, other than being insane, we were directed to follow in the footsteps of the legions many years previous. As we walked in their path, now lit up like a runway, awaiting some craft from outer space. Our steps rang out in the clear night air, we listened, awaiting the sound of an oncoming army, which had long gone.

The moon shone bright, as we climbed, step by step, into the night. Less often did the still night air get rumbled by the purr of a passing car, changing note as it passed, on its way into the distance.

The unending road, set between banks of snow, climbed high over the backbone of Britain. Sparse signs of habitation, the moon sank over the ridge, getting lower, as we reached each new high, untill no more; leaving a single light, like a lantern by the side of the road. Prising the frozen door, gratefull of the heat, we rested in this "mini" communication centre, untill the discomfort overcame the cold.

It was some time before we found a farmer had left a dutch barn, and hay, up in those hills. Like two hedgehogs we burrowed into the hay, untill coming out of hibernation with the rising sun; covered in hay, sparkling all over with sequins of frost, we entered the new day.

As the day brightened, it made us sparkle into hope. The first conveyance slipped slowly, wearing its way with the early news, past us; its dark shape contrasting with the snow. Bob wished he had brought a coat, only his collage scarf wrapped him from the cold. Hands deep in our pockets, we had the sun on our backs, walking away from the chills and hills of the night.

In the early light, the road sign stood;

alone; reminding of mans horror to man; the A6 MURDER; as we stood, frozen to the spot;.....a car quietly slid to a stop, its dark shape shining, chrome gleaming, as if new. Two smartly dressed officers of the law, looked down on us. After telling our story, backed up by our papers; they wished us luck.

As the bright eyed young officers slipped into the distance, hope filled the air. Hope that turned into the return of the little dark van, which looked as if it had been found on a rubbish dump, but as it stopped to offer a ride; touched by fairy dust, a chariot from heaven.

Descending; bundled up with left over news print, we rattled to a hesitant stop, outside a down to earth early morning café; where this jolly, friendly, elderly paper boy, ordered us toast and tea, as we washed the night out of our hair.

Midday; was it time, we could smell the sea, the sun started to fall.....On, or home? Just, one more try, for those last few miles. We chose a shining new 'Jaguar' out of the nonending line of traffic, feeling it was time to give up. The shining moroon limousine glided, with us; swinging into and effortlessly coming to a stop, outside the main entrance of our destination. While our papers were stamped, the station sergent gave us tea, another policeman informed us, we were twentyfour hours behind the only other team to have made it.

An unladen artic, roared south, with the trailer like an aircraft carrier, awaiting the return of its planes. With us on board, by the time we reached 'Brum', our ears were vibrating on their own.

As if prearanged, we were purring down the M.1. in a 'morris minor' estate, sleeping most of the way.

London lights awoke us, as we were pulling into Waterloo Station; minutes later we were pulling out on the last train that night. The only seats, were beside a lecturer and the cook from collage.

By the time we had told them our story, up to the station manager allowing us on the train; we were pulling into Guildford. We were gratefull to share their taxi back to Merrist Wood.

Next morning; our consolation, for being second by two hours, was breakfast! It payed to meet the cook.

I often think back to that small village, not far from Matlock, with its lone centurian.

My Freedon

In its day, siren blaring, lights flashing, life saving transport, painted white, fluorescent stripe, racing, racing, always ready, code name 'Fox', always ready.

Old and tired, siren quiet, standing, standing, rusting, fading, resting, resting. Engine siezed, sinking, where she stood.

Saved from the scrap man; home she came, pulled, yard, by yard, squeaking creaking, against her will, tractor pulling, pulling, yard by yard.

Rebuilt, bit, by bit, step by step, untill, one day, she came to life, with a coat of green, and a cap of red, my freedom she became.

Now a snail, my home from home, twin bedded, two litre, even the kitchen sink. Freedom on four wheels.

Slowly rolling, in a new role, towards her third decade. Quietly passing on her way; sleepily awaiting each new day, to carry me on my way.

As lights flash past, sirens blaring, going another way------

To day.

The motto of Bembridge School

To day is now yesterday, when the train from Waterloo, rattled down the track, untill the old paddle steamer gave us half an half an hour of pitch and heave.

Smoke puffed, on the ride from Ryde, the little steam engine puffed its way, hanging on to an "Era", (only a memory elswhere,) carrying us in carriages; like the rest of the line, built by the victorians. The last few miles, smelling of fumes. The coaches emptied two hundred boys out side the two large wooden gates; behind which stretched an avenue of young horse chestnuts.

The first thing to greet me, those early summer days, as term began, where those young green, finger like leaves, for seven years, marked my progress.

Walking up the drive each building full of memories; just inside the gates, to the right, the art room, where I learned to master the pencil, under the heavy hand of John Mills. After trying to teach me, he gave up, and hid away in the inside of the television.

A few more steps to where I spent the first years at Bembridge; when, not home sick, gardening, needlework, algebra mixed with model boats drifting in the pool; shaded by the chapel; music from the school orchestra, helping the choir to shake the foundations, its square tower facing the refectory on the opposite side of the drive. This red brick building in character with the chapel.

A massive room took up the whole of the first floor, walls lined with books, used for films and talks, "Any Questions" used it one day and old boy another, a young man with a bow tie, a man whos independence got him a knighthood; Sir Robin Day.

Back across the drive, sheltering on the far side of the chapel, was an Elizabethan style building; "New House", its dark beams added to the sinister rule of the cane, which this house had, under the rule of a master, nick named 'Beelzebub'. One side of the house was given over to "Ruskins Gallery", a shrine to Ruskin. I spent one sunday listening to Handel's Messiah, surrounded with painting and letters by Ruskins. The windows looked on down the drive, to a new modern building, that of the headmaster. On we go; passing the cycle sheds hidden in the trees.

A few more yards, standing in the middle of the courtyard. The drive comes to an end, with a round flower bed, right outside whot was known as "Old House". This was where I spent my years in the senior part of the school. A large building, it was in its day, very grand; oak panelled, sweeping staircase off a mosaic floored grand hall. windows on the opposite side, looking out over the sweeping bay a hundred feet belowe, from 'Black Rock' to 'Calver Cliff'.

Below; the blue water, washed the sand with a soothing rhythm at high tide, cleaning the Eastern end of the Island's famous coloured bands of sand, like the end of a rainbow. When the wind came in past 'Nab', a lighthouse five miles out to the East; got up strength; it could send the spray, climbing up the hundred foot cliffs, rising on the wind, up, up, to the open windows of the dormatory on the third floor.

The bell, worked its way up and moved from dorm to dorm, tolling the beginning of a 'New day'. After a wash in cold water; we must have been some of the earliest joggers, down to the main gates and back, half a mile in all; before making a perfect bed, with luck, passed to go for breakfast, down the drive to the refectory. Feeling better for a bowl of porridge, eggs bacon etc., time to cross the drive, to thank the 'Lord' for a new day. Fifteen minutes later, a snake of young men, in green herringbone tweed jackets and grey trousers make their way turning away from the cycle sheds around the gymnasium. A line of two story classrooms and labs, where the young men would spend the next few hours. The far end of these brick buildings was a green timber building, where we learnt dovetail, lathe and other skills in wood; from repairing broken beds to making canoes.

In the little brick room, standing detatched was housed an old press, where the school newspaper was printed. Last, but not least, the squash courts. All these buildings faced out to sea, looking across one of the football fields.

Seventy acres of playing fields; cricket, football, grass track for running, shot javelin, high and long jump; fields and scrub running down to the sea, where swimming, canoeing and other water activities took place in the bay. Horsriding nearby, whilst if you wished to learn to sail, the walk though the village, down to the harbour, along the toll road, was more than worth while, whot better place to be tought than the famous sailing club, Bembridge, renowned worldwide.

From the yatchs bobbing in the harbour, we often walked on the rocks covered in weed, with the waves lapping at our feet, passing lobster pots to the Forelands; were we would sit and watch the budgerigars, in and out of the aviary, Whilst other people fed on lobsters in the Inn. On along the edge of the cliff, only feet above the pounding sea, on past the dark rocks, run out, just under the high tide; at low tide stood like a pier, known as Black Rock. It was from there we swam the 'mile', to the other side of the bay, under the watchfull eye of the school, a hundred feet above. Climbing out under 'Culver Cliff', which went stright up hundreds of feet. It was here, at low tide, with great care we watched the currents meet; sweeping out so strong, to take jetsom miles out to sea.

Scrambling around, below this towering cliff giving its name to the bay; "White Cliff". Rounding the eastern point of the Island into Shanklin Bay. Along, under the cliff as it turned from white to red; now three hundred feet and over-hanging. Just a few feet wide, rugged rocks separated it from the deep water rushing along its base, and on out, out it went, rushing carrying all to that lighthouse, just to be seen, Nab. As you cleared the underside of "Redcliff", sand spread before you, away from danger, sweeping like a cresant moon all the way to the "airmans carrot plot" of the last war; Ventnor Radar Base.

Turning back, just before we reached the road at Sandown, a track led up a steady slope. sheep grazed right to the edge, as you climbed, one hundred, two hundred feet, up and on up; two hundred and fifty, and then three hundred feet. Over the edge, nothing could be seen between you and the sand washed by the waves below. The foundations of an old building, stuck out, waiting for its turn to fall, unbroken to the sea below; rabbits hopped

on it, unaware of the danger.
Moving away from the edge down the slope, the Sea soon vanished, as you met the track I often trod on the cross country run.
The grass airfield, with its bye-planes mixed with a new craft; one that they called a hovercraft, could be seen in the dip of the land, in the distance. Over the stile, where I fell while running for the school, leaving my hand marked for life. On down the slippery slope, towords White cliff Bay, then climbing steadily through the scrub, coming up to the back of old House, through the narrow gap, between the Housemasters home and a room used as the music room.
The Housemaster, acting Head, Mr Steadman gave his all to the boys. I can still feel his compassion, as well as feeling the stripes when I sat down. This was clearest to me one day; talking with him, whilst climbing the stairs, he had been talking to my older brother's best friend on a trip to London, and he was telling me of it. When he stopped to repremand a boy, on the ground floor, for doing something unacceptable, and then carred on talking to me as if nothing had happened. He seemed alway to be there and haveing time for us; each in our own way.
Yesterday at school is still with me, to day.

Written for B.B.C. Wildlife Magazine
Essay Competition March 1991

TOMORROW

Balanced to perfection, the rainbow made a halo over the spreading oak tree. The sun warming the damp ground, gave off the smell of newly ironed linen. Like a waterfall, the starlings came down from the hawthorn hedgerow, to the warm damp soil. The old pony, shaking off the rain from his back, as he made his way from the shelter of the oak. The old brand R.N. became visible, a burnt in scar, from his long gone working days. Quietly he was seeing out his days with his companion.

The sound of a hunting horn; calling, again and again; calling the hounds to war. From under the oak, low comes the fox, swiftly, silently. A fine young dog fox, his red coat shining in the bright sun. As he crossed the field, up went his brush, on his way down to the protection of the farmhouse and the friendly back door.

Birds took to the wing, as the cattle got restless, their ears resembling radar equipment, in their movement, as the hounds came into sight. Although the gate was closed it did not hold back the stampede of cows, vanquished by fear.

As the rainbow faded a storm raged between myself and the invading vandals, to call off their hunting hounds. My storm faded into insignificance back in the farmhouse, as the fox found sanctuary by the back door. The radio gave out; the black gold, oil covering hundreds of square miles of the Gulf. As on the land a little light came from oil lights, burning oil wells, while the black smoke turns day into night. While here by the oil fired aga, the cats safely curl up in their basket.

Out on the farm the pig, looking under the turf, was not going to let anything stop her from looking for food. While in the corner of a field, one of the cows was losing her calf, I was to find out later.

My mind went to the Gulf, that black gold, leaving nothing but death behind. I could have thought of the birds, the fish, other animals, or even man, but all I could see in my mind was black. Black sea, black skies, and a land black with greed. The vision of that black gold choking out life made me sick, ashamed, the thought that I had helped in my small way, to black out the rainbow, to keep me warm. A price far to high to pay, my own greed had helped to black out a continent.

Mending the gate later in the day, I could see the pony resting, watching the clouds going by. The fox was long gone on his way, while the pig had retired to the warmth of her sty, to wait for me, too bring food to her. The cows were still wary of everything, after what had happened. The one that had lost her calf, was looking and mooing, round and round the field. I wondered how many animals were doing the same in the Gulf, looking for their lost ones.

After tucking up the pig for the night, as usual, Lassie and I went to walk the land. Lassie, my collie bitch, with her high sense of awareness, tells me where to look, for the badger, fox or vole. Weaving her way quietly through the cattle as if invisible to them, not even the turn of a head. She stopped by the one, aware something was wrong. Seemed to comfort the pining cow, before going off to the west, towards the blood red sky, from where the hounds had come earlier that day. She returned to my side, satisfied the invaders had retreated. So we made our way back to the farmhouse, leaving the rabbits to come out and graze along side the cows. It would not be long now before the badger is out, rooting around, I thought.

That evening, as the wood burnt in the grate and supper cooked on the oil burner, I was only too aware of the power stations that gave me light. Right on time the pheasant took to the wing and other birds became restless, preceding the double boom of Concorde coming home over Cornwall. The television was about to show how war in the Gulf had been won. Technology, victorious, the mighty fire power of the armies. My mind went blank - where are the white flags for the fish? Killed and deafened by the mine, or the sand lizard, when a ton of high explosive drops from the sky? Who is going to re-build the habitats of a thousand-and-one different creatures? No, they can die in the black gold, discarded by man.

I awoke the following day to a beautiful cornish spring, daffodils dancing in the early mist. The shimmering damp light of dawn, giving a fresh clean feel to a new day. Like the mushrooms in the autumn, now hope seemed to push its way up through the ground. The short grass stands up, clean and bright, with jewels of rain glinting in the early sun. Bare patches of earth in the meadow, show that the badger visited last night. His prints still sharp in the builders sand, where he stopped to play. The buzzard wheeling high over-head, calling his mate. The cows graze at peace, as the rabbits grab another mouthfull, before making for the safety of their burrows, and the fox slinks off to his den. Blackbirds dotted around look for worms in the short damp grass, while the robin finds one, where a badger was rooting last night.

Today there is still hope - the old pony died last night - he would have been 43 years old tomorrow.

Death On The Wind

Fields turn to mud, cold and wet; up comes the wind. Water fills the ditches, across the field, held back hedges, on its way down to the sea. Trees shiver, shaking off the water, leaning, bending, roots straining; as cattle face out of the wind.

Rain again, and again, stops sharp by the window; plays an uneven beat on the glass

Pigs curl up, snuggling in the straw, out of the wind, each trying to get closer, closer to each other. As the roof vibrates, creeks, to hold its own. Birds fill out their feathers, under leaves, holding tight, as if at sea.

Dripping gates, rattled, as the wind forced through the bars; trying again, and again, to force the catch to open. Rabbits, worm and snug, await the sun; leaves blown into the dells, to make shelter for the mice, voals, as spiders cling tight into cracks.

Rain passes, wind weakens, on their way to the Capital. Sun warms the air; cattle squidge, across the field; birds take to wing. Tiles lye, broken, on the ground; fields turned to mud, catch plastic, carried by the wind; to choke; the inquisitive.

The House Jack Rebuilt, and the wall, came tumbeling down.

I rember that winter when the snow lay on the ground, the fox came up to the back door; icicles hung like fairy lights. We drew the curtans tight by night and sat by the fire, as the logs burnt bright.

As usual that morning we fed the animals before collecting fire wood. It was clear, dry, without a breath of wind; Jack Frost was about, the church bell rang out; a dog in the distance barked; clatter, a faraway train went; in the valley the smoke from a cottage, rising slowly to heaven.

Another work, of another Jack was to show that day. The wood by the back door, was to stay. Little did the draughts matter now. From back to front, top to bottom it was no more. No tempest, flood nor mine; just gravity had pulled it to the ground. Stunned; we stood, while the roof did splay; shocked! to the price we had to pay; No part the plans did play. Walls bent and creaked another day.

Christmas came and went behind that canvas wall; no log fire, but the glow of calor gas, to keep us warm; toilet paper to stop the drought, and a mattress on the floor.

Christmas turned into newyear, new snow replaced the old, cattle stood and

stared; paper shuffled, the wind blew; the days got longer, people came and people went, the days got longer. Sheep had lambs; the cattle stared and paper shuffled. The snow melted on telephone wires only to be frozen by the reply. Lines from London became red hot, things began to thaw: The T.V. worked a little better; Thats Life: The telephone whispered; dangerous structure, just rebuilt, paper shuffled. The sheriff sent a deputy, to see; the raft had gone, to see; the plans we did see; thats life.

By the time the lambs had gone, the apples could be seen on the trees and the cottage had a new end; but not the end.

Over the years calves were born, grew up and gave birth; foxs still pass by the back door, the badger has worn a track across the field, swallows came and go as the rent falls due. Drip, drip, drip, reminding us of that Christmas years ago, the cottage still settling inch by inch; Crack! windows do not bend.

No court has heard, that the sheriff knew his man; while paper shuffles slowly now working its way back, to the back of the file, joining the report from the surveying man.

Roses grow over the front door; while swallows nest under the eves; children play in the buttercups; blue-tits dance among the willows; church bells drift on the wind, drip, drip, drip; swallows glide, dive, and climb again; drip, drip, drip. (1983 to 1988 christmas)

A Very Special Day

Just another day?

Cattle feed on hay, daffodills in golden joy, birds sing as if spring has come.

Kathryn's day;

Twenty one, years to the day from when her Uncle, had his Day.

While winter showers blow overhead; trees bud, burst into leaf; sun today, rain tomorrow.

The well of happiness overflows. Days grow longer, my Daughter becomes an Aunt; birds look for a nest. Snapdragons live on and flower again. Not jest another day; yesterday I was in print, today a Grandfather, what tomorrow?

Pigs grunt, dogs bark, as cats hide behind flower pots. The wind rustles the leaves on the Bay tree, as Grandma comes home.

My son, so proud; the girl he loves, now a Mum!

Phones ring East, to the Capital; North to the Penines; up grading Grandparents, to Great Grandparents and on down the Family tree.

The smell of sweet blossom fills the night air; the fragranee of the Babe, full of hope; love, so great, filling every empty space.

Kathryn's day, ... for the rest of the world; just another day.

A Place For Honey

Hills roll down, coloured with spreading oaks, green fields, sheep and cattle. Quietly snuggling, the barn keeps off the rain, white in the sun, cows graze, boats float, glide over the lake, sweeping round disappearing behind the island, swallows glide, and rise again, trout leap, rings ripple, as bees busily gather honey, from the apple trees, hawthorne and clover. Lilies add their beauty to the streams own wild flowers, as dragon flies colour the air.

A buzzard overhead, wild life scurry for shelter.

Trains pass gently by, keeping the North wind at bay. Whilst to the South, the river meanders its way along the Parish boundary willows shade the water, as it babbles its way to the Fal and the sea.

Months of joy spent living in the caravan, whilst the cattle, pigs and sheep grazed; farm tools, stored in the chalet, while we stared to build our home in 1981.

Years have passed, trees have grown, hay fills the barn, rabbits pay, and the oaks still spread their branches, as the hills roll down - - - - - - - -

"Waste Not, Want Not".

This small farm, where the badger takes his place with the wise old owl. Making their home, where the miner once toiled.

Giving way to bracken, gorse and bramble over crevice and mound. Lush grass, grazed by the pony makes a meandering line; for mole and worm to busy themselves, making ready for the summer flower.

In the dell, where man collected his gold, the goat shelters from the gale, and finds a winter salad fit for a king. Out of the wind, the pony looks to find, the feast of tasty minerals in his diet, to keep him fit.

Watching by night, the owl drifts on the up draught of the uneven land, awaiting a meal. Badgers play the night through, as bats dart their way, in a hurry as if they have lost there way.

Come midnight, the field rests; as the county community spends its time finding its wants, on the wast of this small farm.

25-1-89 DM

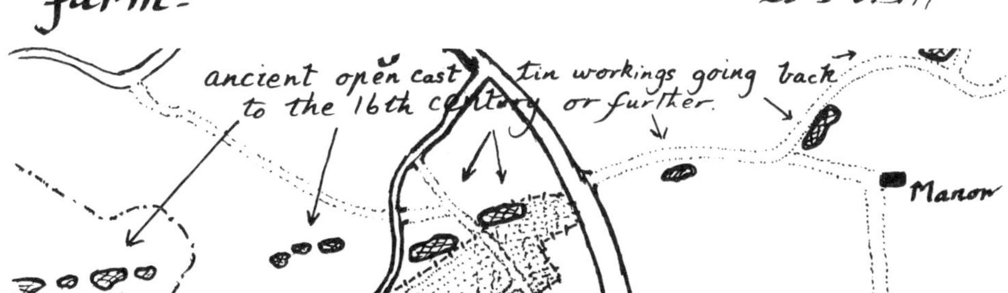

The End of the Rainbow

The pot of gold at the end of the Rainbow, Mother Nature has perfected over millions of years.

Balanced to perfection; to complex for man to comprehend, the wonders it performs.

Discarded and tasty; man's unwanted, left behind. Plastic, rubber and string; like a "Gin Trap", waiting! Often small, unoticed by the eye; to kill, slowly; the inquisitive, looking for a meal. Killing from the inside, the trap is set again; baited for the next.

No wonder, we who work the land, not as a job; not as a living; it is our religion. We fight a holy war; not to spread rubbish in this holy place.

Like a church, you are welcome, please do come and praise the Lord for what you see, the rainbow, bright and clear. See if you can find the pot of gold?

A gold, more brilliant than man has ever mined. No bank, could hold so much; the total wealth of all the world.

If only man could create, just a little of whot a rainbow shows. Sun to keep us warm, water to drink, are but two out of the spectrum, to create the magic of that gold. Each colour, balanced to perfection, bending down to earth; showing us where gold can be found. The spectrum of the Universe showing off the marvels of Nature.

Gold we can twist, to change its shape, make it into liquid or a crown; keep it for ourselves or share it right around. There is the same gold at the end, no matter how thin you pull it, or how thick you make it; it is the same gold in the end.

Over the centuries, man has endeavoured for his own ends, to make and break the secret of that pot of gold. His mind so set, on the gold; he cannot see the gold is Mother Nature, and her pot is the Earth.

The pot of gold, is at the end of the Rainbow.

Letters On Their Way

April has turned to May, the sun and wind have dried the land, the trees burst into leaf. Young, green, leaves like flags, dress the land with the message, Oak before the Ash, we are in for a splash. The badgers track is worn bare, in the lush young grass, dust blows off the hedge, where he nightly strolls; or like a young child playing, slides, recklessly, making his descent.

The grass is kept short, where rabbits nightly feast, on we go, up where the mighty lorry roars, black fumes, blast the dust from the road, into the air. Rain in the air, makes the perfumes more pronounced. Shortly they are replaced by chemicals, meant for the land, drifting on the wind, changing to a sweet smell, of what seems like junket, overcomes the rest. It **maybe** the tin mine nearby.

Counting the spots of rain, the letters placed in the hole in the wall, avoiding the scarce but speeding vehicles, relieved the road is now behind us. Eyes itching with dust, the chemical smells now fade, replaced with the fragrance of the wild life, and the cow.

Opening the kitchen door, roast beef slowly cooking, overcomes all other smells, tempting your tast buds to feast. Within the hour, the heavens open up, rain soaks the dust, the air is filled with a smell, as if the fields have been ironed. Dogs make for cover, as the cattle dance for joy, on their way to shelter, under a nearby tree. Within minutes, the grass refreshed by the passing shower, seems to start growing, as if, it to knows that April has turned to May.

To the Lady I know as "Aunty Peggy",

'My Godmother'

A song of the nightingale,

The music of life, babbles like a brook; sweet soothing notes, loving from the past; memories harmonising with the present

Days long gone, when a slim figure spoke soft; like a mother from heaven. To this small, blond, blue eyed boy. Sweets at Christmas, far more than we deserved. Fireworks, that lit up the 5th of November; each year, but more, much more, her soft firm voice, guiding my way.

A voice from the 'Smoke', not the clouds; but still an Angel, shining a guiding light. A 'Fairy Godmother', her quiet soothing music playing, adding to the love life has given me.

Parents of mine, so loving ..... I didn't deserve a Godmother so sweet, as to leave music, lovingly playing such a sweet tune in my memory.

I have a Nightingale forever with me....

To the Tall Ships

Shaped like an arrow head,
Rising on the tide,
Easing clear of the mud,
Oak and pine, so fine,
Built to work the Scilly Isles,
Now she glides the Fal.

Driven by a 'Handy Billy',
Since nineteen hundred,
Making one more mission,
This time for pleasure,
Over the secrets of the deep,
Out to the ships so tall.

Docks to the right,
Lighthouse to the left,
Heavens above, abyss below,
A ferry passes to and fro,
A coastguard watches, 'Piccadilly Circus',
Floats around 'Trafalgar' this day.

Two naughtical miles,
Out the traffic goes,
Helford passage,
Guarded by a tin frigate,
Dust covers, over the guns,
Now being used as a Royal Grandstand.

Tall ships wait, out of range,
Of the Cavalier, or Roundhead,
Awaiting the single blast,
To lower the square miles of canvas,
To catch the breeze to take them,
Over the edge of the world dropping to the
underside.

Back on the tide,
The engine's steady rhythm,
Like the beating of a drum,
Announcing our return,
As the water rose, on we went
Parting the water with each beat of the drum.

On past the rusty liners,
Tethered to the buoys,
Past the barges, left behind from the war,
Herons scatter as we round the bend,
As we watch each marker buoy,
Up the channel, quietly now.

'Drums' muffled, easing our way,
Sliding on the high tide into our resting place,
As the tide turns;
Sinking slowly into the mud, oak and pine,
Looking back down the cliff in the half light,
We see an arrowhead.... come to rest.

D.M. 1-3-89